Grit for Kids

Grit for Kids

16 top steps for developing
Grit, Passion, Willpower, and Perseverance
in kids for self-confidence
and a successful life

Lee David Daniels

ISBN: 978-1-521109-43-4

Table of Contents

Introduction

I WANT TO THANK AND CONGRATULATE you for reading the book *Grit for Kids*.

"I quit!", "It's so tough!", "You can't make me!"

Is this something you hear on a regular basis from your kids? I know I did. As a proud father of two boys, I heard this way too much. We parents want our kids to succeed and perhaps more importantly, to be able to overcome the inevitable obstacles that will come up. We want our sons and daughters to be resilient and pursue their passions!

I am passionate about the power of grit to transform a person. Ardent interest, focused practice, and perseverance are pillars for the solid stone foundation of success. As a life-long learner and father, I had a strong desire to apply these principles to my sons' life and see them flourish.

The journey began with me going online. I started searching for concise usable information on how to build resilience and grit in children but came up short. I had to search many different sources and speak to more than a few people. This is why I decided to write this book.

Through many hours of research on and off-line and lots of cups of coffee, I assembled a mountain of white papers, case studies, and internet articles. I started a long and daunting task of putting it all together into a comprehensive and actionable book that can be used by any parent, grandparent, uncle/aunt, coach, or anyone who has the privilege of influencing children.

The book is organized in a simple to follow problem/solution format. Each chapter provides scenarios your kids are likely to encounter, steps you can take, and applications of these steps in the real world. I've also included questions you can ask your kids to get their valuable feedback. This enables you to engage and guide them more effectively.

You will learn proven steps and strategies that you can apply immediately to teach your son or daughter to overcome every challenge, come out on top, and learn to develop perseverance, willpower, passion, and a commitment to excellence (a.k.a. Grit) that will help them excel their entire lives.

I am so excited about what I am about to share with you! My wife and I use these techniques to get our kids over hurdles that spring up almost daily. It is challenging but immensely gratifying to help them get over stumbling blocks, one leg at a time. Please visit my blog at www.LeeDavidDaniels.com to see how we do it.

There is so much to say about the topics of grit and parenting that I could not fit it all within the book. Please **SIGN UP** at the site above for free goodies such as real life grit stories, downloaded blog posts, additional resources, and much, much more!

Thanks again for reading this book, I hope you enjoy it!

What is Grit?

Definition

In her book, *Grit: The power of passion and perseverance,* Dr. Angela Duckworth defines grit as the intersection of passion for a purposeful goal and the perseverance to overcome obstacles to achieve that goal. Grit, talent, and all other psychological traits relevant to success in life are influenced by genes and also by experience. There's no single gene for grit, however. Since the purpose of this book is to provide practical how-to advice for developing grit in your kids, I will not delve too deeply into the definition. I do encourage you to read Dr. Duckworth's excellent book for a thorough discussion on the concept of grit.

People that have grit are extraordinarily resilient and are willing to put in the effort to get things done. The reason they are motivated to do so is that they are driven by an overriding purpose. In other words, they are a car traveling on a road and following a map with a destination. Just like on any road trip, detours and slow traffic can happen. Having grit allows people to overcome these obstacles.

Grit is more endurance than strength. Grit is about working on something you care about so much that you're willing to see it through to completion. It is not a chase of one shiny object after another but a commitment to be on a steady course. It helps to think of this concept as a race. A runner that sprints and gets ahead of the pack but then tires and can't finish is not gritty. A runner that quits because of discomfort is not gritty as well. A runner that exemplifies grit is one that runs at a steady pace, sometimes speeding up, sometimes slowing down, but eventually getting to the finishing line.

Sticking with an activity after a particularly tough day is another example of grit. Picture your child who plays soccer and had a particularly hard time scoring a goal or making a pass during a crucial game. That is devastating. If that child comes back the next day ready to give 100% effort, that kid is just glowing with grit.

Perhaps, the following quotes show the spirit of grit.

"I'm going to do it, I don't care how", "I will find a way!"

Relationship between talent, grit, and achievement

Dr. Duckworth provides the following equation to explain this relationship. For the mathematically challenged, don't worry, it's not complex!

$$\text{Talent} \cdot \text{Effort} = \text{Skill} \quad \text{Skill} \cdot \text{Effort} = \text{Achievement}$$

Talent is how quickly your skills improve when you apply effort. Achievement is what happens when you take your acquired skills and perfect them. Talent matters but you will notice that effort is in both equations. Effort builds skill and effort accelerates skill into achievement.

Effort is very apparent in an exercise routine. Having sore muscles after lifting weights but trudging to the gym the following day, ready to try again, is showing effort. Why, you might ask? When you don't come back the following day and completely back out of a commitment to getting in shape, guess what happens to effort? Yes, effort will be a big fat zero. As a result, your skill in weightlifting will not improve and whatever skill you have acquired will be useless.

Effort overshadows talent. Greatness is attainable. Greatness is multiple small achievements built over a period of time. I like to think of this in terms of ancient Egyptians. They worked for years with primitive tools to raise pyramids that tower over the vast desert. The laborers built them one stone at a time. Each floor was a small achievement, each a step in the right direction. This continued until one day, the top stone was put in place and the workers looked around the flowing sands in triumph.

Developing Grit

Per Dr. Duckworth, there are two ways to grow your grit. The first is "inside out" by developing interests, deliberate practice, and connecting your activities to a greater purpose. The second is growing grit from the "outside in" which involves parents, uncles, aunts, teachers, coaches, and others. This second method requires setting appropriate challenges while supporting your kids psychologically, encouraging participation in extracurricular activities for more than 2 years, and immersing them in a culture of grit.

Developing Grit from the inside

The process of developing grit goes like this. First, comes interest in an activity. Next comes the capacity to practice that activity by consistently eliminating flaws. To be gritty is to resist being OK with the level of current performance. Gritty people do what it takes to get better no matter how good they currently are now. Third is purpose which I interpret as an activity that is personally interesting and for the benefit of others. Finally, there is expectation of success based on applied effort which I interpret as the ability to keep going when things get difficult.

The key driver of developing Grit in your kids is passion for an activity. Help your children in discovering their passion and increase their chance for success by developing top-level goals. A top-level goal is something your child does just because he wants to. It is the end destination on the map. Becoming a world class violinist is an example.

Mid-level goals are made up of several low-level goals. They are stepping stones on the way to the top-level goal. Think of them as being the planned stops on a map as you edge closer to your destination. Being accepted to a top music school would be an example.

Low level goals are short term and very specific. They are the mile markers on your way to the planned stops. Practicing to play a difficult music piece until perfection would be an example. Thus, all low level and mid level goals must lead to the top level goal.

What one thing do gritty winners do to tie it all together?

In extremely gritty folks, most mid-level and low-level goals are there for the purpose of achieving the desired top-level goal.

Now, on to encouraging passion. Does it make sense to encourage kids to go out and do what they love? Research shows that people are extremely more satisfied when they do something that fits their personal passions. While nobody is fascinated with everything, everyone is fascinated with something. Most successful people spend a long time discovering several different pursuits, and the one that they develop a passion for wasn't more than a passing interest at first.

That said, having kids quickly change activities like old clothes may not be the best option. There are a lot of benefits of sticking it out with something new. A lot of things seem not fun until your child starts getting into it and realizes there are a lot of fun little things to learn and challenging problems to solve. Passion is a little bit of trying different things, followed by a lot of learning, and then a lifetime of mastery. It is extremely important that the initial activation of interest in the child must be followed by many later events that reignite interest. Finally, people in your kids' lives need to be encouraging and supportive of their passions.

Great! So now your kids are interested in an activity. What's next? Practice, practice, practice. Practice grows incrementally. At first, when the skill level is new, it requires a lot of effort in learning it. As your child is learning a lot of fundamental things, the learning curve will be steep. As they develop mastery, the learning curve will flatten and they will learn nuances and how to make what they're already good at even better. It takes thousand upon thousand hours to master something.

Struggle > progress > confidence to try something harder

While your kids could be running around the soccer field until they collapse, this will not necessarily improve their game. How do world class athletes, scientists, and musicians practice? They strive to improve specific problems they are having. They seek out challenges that are just out of reach. Then with unbelievable focus and great determination, world class performers achieve their goals. What follows the conquering of a stretch goal? Yes, you guessed it. It's setting up and striving for a new stretch goal. Like millions of raindrops can form a river, these stretch goals eventually produce world class results.

Once interest is established and a determined practice regimen is put in place, what helps kids to be grittier in the long term is purpose to serve others. Purpose can be a huge motivator because your children will know that they're not just doing an activity to help themselves. They will know they are benefitting others too. For example, Ryan Hreljac, a Canadian kid, was shocked to learn that children in Africa had to walk many miles a day just to get clean water. By doing chores and public speaking, he financed a well in a Ugandan village. His effort and determination led to Ryan's Well Foundation which brings access to clean water to more than 714,000 people.

If passion, practice, and purpose are the foundations of grit, optimism is the glue that keeps them together.

In a study done by Marty Seligman, it was discovered that optimists usually look for fleeting and precise causes of their setbacks, while pessimists accept that lasting and inescapable causes are the cause. Aaron Beck found that our feelings and behavior are formed by our interpretation of events, not what actually happened.

Optimism, or downplaying negativity, as it relates to grit is the idea that it's your children's efforts that will make their top goal come true. It's not that "I really think that my goal will come true" but "my efforts will make my goal come true". Lady luck is completely out of this equation.

Here is an example from Dr. Duckworth's life. She enrolled in a neurobiology class and did not do well in the class at first. She took a quiz and a mid-term exam and failed. Her professor's teaching assistant advised her to drop the course. Despite this setback, she resolved to not only pass the class but to major in neurobiology. "I won't quit! I can figure this out!" She did extra work and practiced resolving test problems under time pressure. This allowed her to brilliantly pass the final exam and the class.

I had a similar situation in my life. I grew up in a time when personal computers were just starting to be affordable for the average American. I was hooked and wanted to become a computer programmer. I first tried in my first year of High School and failed miserably. I had the lowest grade in my class. I tried again in two years and got an average grade, not good, not bad. The same teacher advised me to give up computers as it was not my thing. Well, years went by and I became a well-paid computer programming professional for many years. I accomplished this feat with passion and lots of persistent practice ironing out my coding skills.

Growing Grit from the outside

If growing grit from the inside is like a plant that grows due to its capacity to absorb nutrients, growing grit from the outside involves placing that plant in good soil, a sunny location, and regularly watering it. When it comes to your kids, this involves giving them progressively harder tasks, getting them involved in extracurricular activities, and getting them surrounded by gritty people.

Psychologist Robert Eisenberger ran a study where he divided two groups of kids and gave them tasks to do. Both groups had to do a series of tasks for which they received monetary rewards. One group got progressively more difficult tasks each time they succeeded. The other group did tasks with the same difficulty level as before. Then both groups were given a different task, copying words to a sheet of paper. The children that did the harder tasks worked harder than those that did tasks at the same level. The conclusion of this experiment is that without understanding that effort leads to reward, kids can revert to laziness.

Angela Duckworth has found that kids who are involved in activities outside of school for more than one year "earn better grades, have higher self-esteem, and are less likely to get in trouble." Furthermore, kids that stick it out for more than two years have been shown to be able to hold a job and make more money. The key is to have children sign up for an activity for one year, sign up again for another year and make some progress in between.

Dr. Duckworth refers to a practice in her family called the 'hard thing rule'. This means that everyone in the family has to do a hard thing. First, the definition of hard in this case means that the activity requires purposeful practice. Second, quitting is allowed as long as it occurs at an organic point such as the end of the season, end of the sports camp, or some other natural event. Finally, the hard thing must be chosen by you or your child. No one should choose it for you.

In our family, my son chose playing piano as his hard thing. My wife was very excited about this and we signed up for an 8-week lesson plan. We drove him to the lessons and listened patiently as he played twinkle twinkle little star over and over. Despite many hours of purposeful practice, he just was not interested. There were plenty of bad days where he threw a tantrum and didn't want to practice but we did not let him stop. Finally, we allowed him to quit, but not before the 8 weeks were completed. Why did we allow him to quit, you might ask? The answer is that he's young and should explore many interests before settling. Music is just not one of them right now.

Find a place with a gritty culture for your children. Have them join and watch as the culture overtakes them and makes them grittier. The higher the standard of the culture, the more intense the need of those already on the team to keep those standards high. Joining a culture of grit has a benefit of motivating your children to keep going even when in the short term they would rather give up.

My friend's son belongs to a local baseball team. Baseball is his passion but even so, he sometimes slides toward mediocracy. Last year, a new head coach was hired. He encouraged everyone to try as hard as possible often providing awards and lunches to the team. He took mistakes as lessons learned for the entire team. The effect was that the individuals on the team slowly raised expectations of themselves and that in turn made for a grittier and higher performing team.

The importance of a progressive mindset

Growth Mindset for kids, as defined by Carol Dweck, means that children can change if given the right opportunity and support, if you try hard enough, and if you believe you can do it. In contrast, a Fixed Mindset means that while your children can learn a new skill, their capacity to learn cannot be expanded. The difference between these mindsets comes in when your kids hit a bump in the road, a setback. Then, a person with a fixed mindset will become discouraged because they will believe that they can't learn what it takes to overcome the setback. A person with a growth or progressive mindset will believe that they can learn something new to overcome the obstacle.

How can your child overcome a fixed mindset? Give praise when they accomplish a task with effort. Praise them when they truly accomplish something difficult. Provide support for them to achieve their goals.

A key to developing a progressive mindset is optimistic self-talk. What a lot of high-performing athletes and musicians do is a morning affirmation. This is simply saying to yourself every morning that you can overcome the hurdles that will inevitably come your way. Kids can be taught to do this as well. It's a simple but very powerful tool.

Statements that encourage mindset and grit.

Discourages growth and grit	Encourages growth and grit
You've got talent!	You've put in amazing effort!
You gave it a good shot. Better luck next time.	You gave it your all but it still didn't work. Would you like to sit down to see what you can fix for next time?
This is too hard for you.	This is hard for you right now. With some practice, it will become easier.
This activity is just not for you	I know you can do this activity. You know I'm there to support you.

Why should you encourage Grit?

Now that you have a good understanding of what grit is, why should you care? I mean, as a parent, you have plenty of things to occupy your time.

The reason to encourage grit is simply that it's one of the key factors that will drive your child's success and resilience in the years to come. There are so many benefits that it could take up another whole book just to list and describe them. For the purpose of this book, we will cover just the most prominent ones below.

- To foster effort over talent so that kids understand that their current ability can be improved and formed into mastery
- To encourage calculated risk taking so that children can reach for their dreams without having a paralyzing fear of failure
- To benefit others by converting your kids' interests and purpose into actions to improve your community
- To allow you, their parents, coaches, mentors, to have the privilege of demonstrating grit in the face of adversity
- To give your children the skills and mental resilience to withstand whatever life throws their way in school and beyond

To foster effort over talent

"Hard work beats talent when talent doesn't work hard."
                                        – Tim Motke

The vast amount of research says that if students are talented, we begin to lavish attention on them and hold them to higher expectations. We expect them to excel and that expectation becomes a self-fulfilling prophecy. Fostering high expectations at any talent level is sure to spur a greater effort in your kids.

Attempting to do tasks they're not quite good at, not getting results they wanted, and learning what they need to improve is exactly the way world-class performers practice. Feelings of frustration and wishing they could do things better are a normal reaction in purposeful practice. Practice to eliminate areas of weak performance should be encouraged at every opportunity. In doing something over and over again, something that was never natural becomes almost second nature.

To encourage calculated risk taking

Risk seems to be a bad word. When we hear it or think of it, we start getting a knot in our stomachs. Why? We know failure can come with taking risks and that causes us stress just thinking about it. Your kids need to learn how to use stress as a springboard for overcoming setbacks and by so doing, learn to take calculated risks.

Scientists explain it this way. There are primitive low order centers in the brain, like the amygdala, that respond to negative experiences. As we handle stress and overcome obstacles, we are teaching our pre-frontal cortex that we can handle challenges. When we encounter the next challenge, our pre-frontal cortex moderates the message sent by the amygdala and calms us down. This in turn allows us to overcome the obstacle.

When do kids learn to fear failure? It happens earlier than you think. Before they even get to first grade, they begin to realize that their blunders invoke certain reactions in adults.

What do the adults do? We wrinkle our brows. We hurry over to our little boys and girls to let them know that they've messed up. What are we teaching them? Humiliation, anxiety, and disgrace. Kids learn that not succeeding is bad, really bad. To protect their feeling of self-worth, they will learn to not take risks and stop striving to be their best.

What can you do? Try what studies have proven to be effective, emotion-free mistake making modeling. Commit an error on purpose and let your kids catch you while at it, then model the correct way to prevent the mistake.

For example, let's say your child is learning how to be organized and to not forget their homework at school. After coming home from work, you can say to your kid, "I forgot my notebook at home because I was rushing to work. I wish I would have written a reminder on my calendar. I'll do that now so that I don't forget it tomorrow."

To benefit society

Just like Ryan Hreljac, the kid whose efforts brought clean water to a Ugandan village, the interest, purpose, and effort your child can put forth can have benefits way beyond your family. We all want to make an impact, so imagine how incredibly satisfied your kids will be if their efforts lead to improving the lives of others. You can play a part in this by encouraging grittiness in your children.

David Yeager, a prominent psychology professor, recommends reflecting on how the work a person is already doing can make a positive contribution to society. I like to think that applies to kids as well. If your child is involved in coaching younger kids in their favorite sport or tutoring kids in a subject after school, they are directly benefitting society. Why? The children they help will improve and by doing so, they in turn will be more productive and happier. In some cases, the kids your child helped will help others become better.

This will trigger a worthy cycle of benefit. The effects are multiplied because we enrich each other's lives.

To be your kids' role model

Your kids look up to you, their parents, more than anyone else, period. While peers have influence, mom and dad's opinion matters most, even when they don't admit it. If you are reading this and are not a parent but are a coach or teacher, your influence is very imperative. Kids want to and will look up to you.

For example, Angela Duckworth watched her mother help many other people throughout her life. This made her see firsthand the power of purpose. I watched my parents immigrate to the United States and struggle with learning the English language. This served as an inspiration to me. My best friend had a math teacher that encouraged him to purposefully practice algebra until he couldn't look at a math problem anymore. That patience paid off as my friend learned and passed the class. More importantly, the teacher's efforts had a lasting effect as my friend learned that with focused practice, he could improve on almost anything.

So if you're a parent, you're probably struggling with how to structure your parenting style so that it's both supportive and demanding. In other words, is grit made by enforcing mercilessly high standards or is it incubated in the soft blanket of unconditional support? The answer it seems is a bit of both.

There are four parenting styles: neglectful, permissive, authoritarian, and authoritative. I will not waste your time with the ones that don't work. The one that produces grittier and happier kids is the authoritative parenting style.

In the authoritative style of parenting, the kids are supported with love, reasonable limits on behavior, and encouragement of dreams. Kids are also held to a high standard to achieve their goals by overcoming fears and not quitting. The authority of the parents is based on understanding and being wise.

Children have within them seeds of interest and their own ability. It's up to us as parents to nurture these abilities and be responsive to their needs.

One caveat here is to make sure the final decision of whether something should be pursued is your child's and not yours. Make sure you're not pushing them to be like you, or making them follow your dreams and goals. Ultimately, it should be their goals that you hold the high standard to.

A key benefit of authoritative parenting is that your kids will start to respect and try to be more like you. They will do this because of your support, respect for them, and high standards that you hold them to.

Amy is an example of an authoritative parent. Her daughters are both enrolled in ballet and have been tempted to quit several times. She has refused to let them because she believes they are more than capable at excelling at dance. Instead, she lends an ear and shoulder for them to voice their frustrations, then finds them the resources to improve their skills.

Ask yourself, how much purpose and grit you have for your own goals. Then examine if your parenting style inspires your child to imitate you. If the answer to the first question is "a lot," and you find your child copying your best habits, congratulations! You're already parenting for grit.

As important as parenting style is, don't forget to exude optimism and downplay negativity. Your kids see your attitude every day and will learn to emulate it. A study found that optimistic teachers were grittier and happier and were more effective in getting the most from their students. As caretakers for your children, you should strive to make yourself grittier and happier. When you keep searching for ways to change your situation for the better, you will eventually find them. When you stop searching or believe solutions do not exist, you guarantee failure.

To plant the seeds of success for school and beyond

Growing grit requires pushing your kids' out of their comfort zone just a bit so that the task at hand is achievable but requires a bit more effort than a child is used to. Grit developed at a young age grows and becomes stronger as a person becomes an adult.

Benjamin Bloom, a psychologist, noticed a three-phase progression to mastery of their field. The first were the "early years" where interest develops, next were the "middle years" where the purposeful practice produces results. The last and longest period are the "later years" where "purpose and meaning" of work becomes obvious.

Kids who see their interests as a higher purpose as opposed to just a chore have been proven to be most satisfied with their interests and life overall. How your child sees any particular school subject is very important. For example, a child can see school as a job, something they need to do like walking and talking. They could see it as a stepping stone to higher things such as the progression from primary school to middle school, to high school. On the other hand, they can see school as a calling for education, a foundation for life-long learning in school and beyond.

The best way to encourage grit, it seems, is by encouraging your kids to get involved with something that benefits themselves and others at the same time. In studies that followed kids for two years, it has been shown that children that were doing an activity with both self and other oriented motives mentioned that schoolwork was more meaningful. As the people that guide and nurture your children, you can cultivate interest in activities that accomplish both motives.

Study after study has shown that purpose is a powerful motivator. "I can make a difference" is a phrase that propels a kid to achieve great things. A child needs to believe that their efforts are not useless. Once that belief is set, many great things are possible.

Another reason for you to encourage grit is to teach your children to use stress to their advantage.

Is stress bad? Not always. A study by Steve Maier showed that rats that dealt with stress that they can control are able to deal with stress better later in life. They became resilient. In contrast, rats that had stress that they had no control over became helpless. Our kids are not rats of course but the same principle applies. Children that learn to overcome stress become more resilient and no longer feel helpless later in life.

Now that you have learned what grit is and why you should encourage it, let's dive into the building blocks of building grit. The rest of this book will provide you with the tools you need to build a gritty and ultimately successful and happy child.

Encourage Passion

THE DIFFERENCE BETWEEN ENDURANCE AND grit is passion. Endurance is putting one foot ahead of the other to get a task done. Grit or perseverance is the ability to overcome setbacks to achieve your goals. Our role as parents is to help our kids figure out exactly what they care about enough to get it done while overcoming the inevitable obstacles that will come their way.

Jose, a tall enthusiastic teenager was always jumping from one activity to another. One month it was baseball, the second soccer, the third karate. He would be fired up about it in the beginning then as the routine set in, he would lose his enthusiasm. At the end of the day, he would beg his parents to quit.

Steps you can take

- Make it a part of your routine to encourage the kids to try something new.
- Talk to them to understand what their interests are, then encourage them to pick what they are really excited about and give it a try
- Pick an activity and do it with them. Then talk about how it felt for them. Tell them how it was for you. Did you like it? Did they? Were they discouraged when it got hard or were they "fired up" about it?

Applications in the real world

Jose's parents sat him down and asked him questions about each activity he tried. They observed how he described each one. He used words like "it's ok" "not bad", and "whatever" to describe all the sports he tried. Then they asked him what he liked to play most with his friends or his two brothers. His eyes lit up when he described how much fun it was to play pickup football after school and to wrestle with his younger siblings. His parents suggested he try football and wrestling in the fall.

Melanie's parents spent each Saturday afternoon trying new things with her. They went ice-skating, they went to see shows, they went to museums, and even rock-climbing. Each car ride home they spoke with her about what she liked about each activity. After seeing one particularly funny play, Melanie couldn't stop talking about it. She went on and on about how great the actress was and how she made her laugh. That summer, her parents enrolled her in an acting camp.

David was constantly spending time counting to one thousand and showing off his skill at solving math problems. When asked by his parents what his favorite school subject is, he said math without any hesitation. His parents signed him up for an extracurricular advanced math after school program which he started attending with great enthusiasm.

QUESTIONS TO ASK YOUR KIDS

- If you stayed home from school, what would you do?
- What would you like to try this weekend?
- I heard your friend has tried (activity). Would you like to try it as well?
- You seem to be really having fun with (activity). What is it about (activity) that makes it fun?
- You don't seem to be enjoying (activity). What about (activity) do you not like?
- I'd like us to try something new this weekend. Why don't we try (activity) together?
- Well, we both tried (activity). What did you like about it the most?

- What did you not like about (activity)?
- Is there anything about (activity) that would make it more fun?
- Would you like to try (activity) again?

Teach Self-Control

THE ABILITY TO STAY RESILIENT is very much dependent on managing the negative emotions that will spring up for your children as they attempt to reach their goal. The urge to stray from a goal for a quick diversion is also very strong during childhood. This chapter will provide you with tools to teach your kids to recognize and manage their negative (and positive) emotions, and to strengthen their impulse control muscles.

Paresh is a very bright child who studies hard every day and is an avid video game player. He is striving to achieve his goal of acing the state math tests. Unfortunately, he frequently gives into the temptation of playing video games into the wee hours making it harder to concentrate in school.

Daniel is a sweet kid who laughs a lot and is conscientious about his performance on the soccer team. He gets very upset when he makes a mistake or perceives that someone has slighted him. His frequent angry outbursts make it very hard for his coaches and teammates to deal with him. He could have a meltdown for a reason as simple as missing a pass or not scoring.

Steps you can take

- Congratulate your children when they show proper control of their impulses
- Help them understand the consequences of their emotions and decisions

- When things get hot, teach them how to recognize and manage their emotions
  - Practice with them so that they become aware of how they are feeling: the fast breathing, the clenched fists, the high pitched voice
  - Have them take ten deep breaths and think about anything except what is stressing them out
  - After they calm down, have them describe exactly what the issue is
  - Talk it through with them so that they understand that most of the time it really is not a big deal.
  - Focus the conversation on the goal at hand and what is going right
  - Move on to another topic

Applications in the real world

Paresh's parents started monitoring him closely to understand where he loses focus and reaches for the game tablet. At that point, they gently reminded him that he still had some homework to finish. They explained that video games, while entertaining, are a distraction from his goal of getting top marks on the math tests. They asked him "What will happen to your test scores if you play every night?" After a few days and more than a few pitched battles, they noticed that when Paresh reached for the tablet, he usually stopped himself and went back to doing his homework. They lavished praise on him for having controlled the urge to play. In a few weeks' time, he stopped playing all together during the week, all of his own accord.

Daniel's parents took Daniel to the park one weekend and had a talk with him. They spoke with him about the importance of recognizing and managing his emotions. They had him recite a recent scenario where he missed a shot on goal and saw a smirk on the face of his teammate. Daniel recognized that his first reaction was clenching his fists and breathing shallowly. He then cursed at the other boy and ran off the field. His parents taught him a better way. They discussed the importance of taking breaths, and after calming down, reflecting that the minor setback is not a big deal. They also made up a sign that had three sentences on it: "Stop" "Breathe" "Move On". The next week after the sit down in the park, Daniel had a tournament game. Around halftime, he missed a pass and saw a teammate shake his head. Sure enough, his adrenaline spiked and he started getting angry. A quick look at his parents and the sign they made up, made him calm down enough to continue playing. Months later, his outbursts became negligible and he is now much closer to becoming the soccer player he wants to be.

QUESTIONS TO ASK YOUR KIDS

- Wow, you really kept your cool. Why do you think you were able to do that?
- Looks like your emotions got the better of you. What made you lose it?
- You seem tense. What are you thinking about?
- What are you feeling right now?
- What is your body doing right now?
- Can you think of something that made you happy today?
- What actually happened (describe situation)?
- Now that you're calm, do you think what happened was a big deal? Why?
- What else is going on? (ask when ready to divert to another topic)

Downplay Negativity

D EVELOPING GRIT IS NOT EASY work. There will be people who will bring your kids down either by making fun of them, downplaying their goals, or being just plain negative. Kids themselves are just developing mentally and will sometimes be down on themselves for failures large and small. In this chapter, we will explore the ways in which to minimize negativity in your children and the people they come in contact with.

Tammy is a sharp and assertive girl who knows what she wants and goes for it with gusto. She wants to be a cheerleader and doesn't miss a game in order to study her role models. Some of her friends however, snicker at the thought of her being a cheerleader. She's too short they say. There's too many prettier, and taller girls. Tammy slowly started to believe this and started getting frustrated. She even started questioning her ability to achieve the goal.

Olivia is an aspiring artist. She paints wild landscapes of bright flowers and tall castles. It is her passion and goal to become a better artist. She often gets frustrated by her perceived inability to grasp a painting technique and even quits painting for periods of time.

Steps you can take

- Teach them to not to get dragged down by negative people. Explain that other people are negative because of their own issues and problems, not your children's.
- If the negative people in your children's life are bringing them down after your conversation, minimize or stop contact with these haters.
- Explain to your children how important it is to visualize achieving their goal. Make them feel how satisfying it will be. This will help them overcome the objections of any naysayers.
- Manage their frustration with shortcomings by explaining that temporary setbacks are natural and expected. Have a conversation with them about the abilities they have to achieve their goal and how far they have gone so far.

Applications in the real world

Tammy's mom went shopping with her after school. As they sat in the food court, they talked about her desire to become a cheerleader. Tammy recited how she was great at gymnastics and how she knew every cheer by heart. They also talked about how one of her friends was particularly doubtful that Tammy can make the squad. As they talked about this friend, they slowly came upon the realization that she had an older sister that tried out and failed to join the cheerleading team. She tried and was not picked. Could it be that the friend was projecting her failures on Tammy? Months went by and Tammy slowly stopped hanging out with her negative friend. Her doubts started to melt away and at the start of the next year, she made the cheerleading team. Next year she is planning to run for captain.

Olivia's dad took her out to dinner and they had a heart to heart talk. They talked about how she started painting as a small child and how frustrated she was at not being able to paint within the lines. They laughed about it. They spoke about how she first learned to mix paints and her frustrations of getting the color wrong. They chuckled over goofy art teachers and how hard it was to draw her first castle. Slowly, Olivia realized how many obstacles she overcame to get to this point. He asked her to articulate how it would feel to be an accomplished artist with her own show at an art gallery. She glowed at the thought of her work getting acclaim. She left that night inspired and not questioning her abilities. Olivia realized that there would be many temporary frustrations but the ultimate prize awaited her if she persevered.

Questions to ask your kids

- What did (name of negative person) say to you?
- Do you believe (name of negative person) is right? Why?
- Why do you think (name of negative person) said this to you?
- Do you think (name of negative person) had a reason to be negative about something that had nothing to do with you?
- What can you do to minimize being around (name of negative person)?
- Are there supportive friends that you can hang around more?
- What do you think it will be like when you achieve (goal)?
- Will you care what (name of negative person) said when you achieve (goal)?
- I'm sorry about (the setback). Do you think it's as bad as you think? Why?
- How has (the setback) affected the way to your goal?
- You've already done (name their successes on the way to the goal). Do you really think (setback) is such a big deal?

Teach Self-Respect

BUILDING PERSEVERANCE IN YOUR CHILDREN is almost impossible unless they respect themselves as people who are worthy and capable of achieving success. They need to be able to protect their interests by being assertive. The steps in this chapter will build your toolkit to achieve self-respect and assertiveness in your children.

Zhu is a cautious child with a slight build, big eyeglasses, and a quiet demeanor. Although he plays tennis quite well, he is shy in other areas. He is prone to have kids pick on him. Sometimes they taunt him with words, sometimes they get physical. Over time, he has started to doubt his self-worth which in turn started affecting his confidence and performance in school and at play.

Tommy is a demanding kid at home, asking his parents to get him food, asking his little brother to fetch his shoes. However, outside his house, he is as quiet as a mouse. He lets other kids get ahead of him in line, he doesn't voice his opinion, and accepts whatever comes his way whether he likes it or not.

Steps you can take

- Tell them how unique they are. Your children are one of a kind. There will never be another, so tell them that.

- Help them to recognize their strengths and special talents. Each child will have something they're good at. Talk to them to identify it and make them understand that this is their special gift.
- Help them to be aware of their weaknesses. Conversely, each child may not be so good doing certain things. They need to be aware of that but make sure not to berate your kids for these shortcomings. Instead, tell them that it is natural to all humans including you, their parent.
- Teach them assertiveness. It's important for them to make their opinions and beliefs then stand by them. Remember, assertiveness is not aggressiveness. Aggressiveness is pursuing your children's interests at the expense of the other person. Assertiveness is pursuing her interest while respecting the needs of the other.
- Tell them you love them unconditionally. This is perhaps the most important step you can take to build a foundation for your children's grit. When times get hard, they will know that you have their back no matter what.

Applications in the real world

Zhu's parents were worried about not only his low self-confidence but also about him being bullied at school. They told him they loved him more than anything and they wouldn't want him any other way. Then they sat down and went over his strengths and weaknesses, opportunities and threats (SWOT). It turned out that Zhu is an excellent tennis player with plenty of potential. He is afraid of conflict however, and this makes him a target of bigger and meaner kids. To boost his self-esteem, his mom and dad told him to focus on his success at tennis and told him "If you can be this great at tennis, you can achieve other things as well." "Those kids can't do what you can, so what right do they have picking on you." The bullying required more work. They needed to get the principal and Zhu's teachers involved. They also enrolled Zhu in a self-defense course for kids. Today Zhu is focused on his tennis and making himself more self-confident. He can also stand up for himself when he needs to. For the most part, other kids leave him alone.

Tommy's dad had a heart to heart with him and asked how it's possible that he is so assertive at home and meek outside. After a few moments, Tommy replied that he is actually quite afraid of conflict and this makes him angry at himself. He takes this anger out on his family by being extra demanding. Having gotten to the bottom of the issue, Tommy's dad told him how it's ok to have weaknesses and how he had the same fear of conflict as a child. He told Tommy how lucky he was to have him as a son and how one of a kind he was. He instructed Tommy how important it is to stand up for himself and that he is no less important than the other kids. Tommy got a step-by-step assertiveness plan book at the library and read it cover to cover. He discussed some strategies with his dad and tried them out. Slowly, he started asserting himself. He would not let others talk over him, cut in front of him in line, or otherwise demean him. Over time, Tommy also became less demanding at home, making him much more of a joyful family member.

QUESTIONS TO ASK YOUR KIDS

- Did I ever tell you that you're one of a kind?
- Do I ever tell you how good you are at (name their strength)?
- What do you think you are really good at? (when they don't know their strength)
- Why do you think you are good at (name their strength)?
- What do you think you need to work on to make it better?
- How can you improve (name of weakness)?
- Did you know that I also struggled with (name of your weakness)?
- You really stood up for what you believe in. Why do you think you were able to do that?
- It seems as though you backed down during (situation). What prevented you from standing your ground?

- What could you do next time to better protect your interests?
- You seemed to be very aggressive during (situation). Do you think (the other person's) interests were respected?
- Did I tell you I love you no matter what?

Teach Respect for Others

RESPECT FOR OTHERS AND EMPATHY are key components for developing perseverance in your children. By understanding what someone else is feeling, your children will learn to build longer and deeper relationships. They will relate to others' struggles in order to draw parallels to their own, enabling them to learn from mistakes. No one succeeds on their own. Your kids will need a support network to thrive. The tools in this chapter allow you to teach them to build this network.

Ellen has a child with a walking disability in her class. She avoids her whenever she can. She will intentionally take a seat at the opposite end of the cafeteria. She will do whatever she can, not be teamed up with her during class projects. On some occasions, she will even taunt the disabled child.

Tyler has a best friend that he's been inseparable from for a number of years. Lately however, they have not been speaking to each other. This makes Tyler sad but he has stubbornly stayed away from his friend.

Nia lives in a busy metropolitan area which has a sizeable homeless population. She is very scared of any homeless person she meets and doesn't understand why anyone would be living on the street.

Steps you can take

- Explain differences in people directly but in a simple manner
- Help them understand their relationships with their friends
- Teach them to right the wrongs they have done to others
- Show them how to thank someone with actions, not just words
- Volunteer with them to be a part of the community

Applications in the real world

Ellen's parents had a talk with her after school. They explained that her disabled classmate is in a wheelchair because a part of her body does not work. They empathized the fact that she is very capable in other ways. For instance, she is quite good at her schoolwork. They asked Ellen if she can try to be the girl's friend instead. After a few unsuccessful days, they had to involve Ellen's teacher. The teacher told Ellen that the girl with the disability likes the same music as Ellen. The next day, Ellen reluctantly approached her and started a tentative conversation about the music group. Little by little, they warmed the ice. Ellen's parents asked her how she could make up for the teasing. Ellen apologized for taunting the girl and offered a download of the latest album so they can listen together.

Tyler's parents encouraged him to explore why he didn't speak with his best friend anymore. They asked if he said anything that made Tyler feel sad? They asked Tyler what he missed most about his friend. The enquired if Tyler's friend did something to him? It turned out that the dispute that put a fissure in the friendship had to do with a baseball game. Tyler's friend insisted that he cheated while sliding to 3rd base. Tyler called him a liar and it escalated from there. The questions Tyler's parents asked, forced him to realize that he really liked his friend for making him laugh and being an avid baseball fan just like him. With some gentle encouragement, Tyler approached his friend for a do-over. They've been inseparable for the entire school year.

Nia's mom talked to her and tried to build empathy for the people who don't have a home to call their own. She reminded her that we are all human beings and that no one is immune to being down on their luck. She arranged for both of them to volunteer at the local food kitchen. There they met and spoke with a few homeless people including a mom and her daughter. Seeing these people as humans and not obstacles on the sidewalk made Nia much more empathic to the plight of others. Volunteering also made her feel she was a part of something bigger. This allowed her to deviate from the self-centered view that kids sometimes have. It also made her realize how lucky she was to have a strong supportive mom.

QUESTIONS TO ASK YOUR KIDS

- What makes you uncomfortable about this person?
- How are you and this person similar?
- Why do you think (friend/teammate/classmate) likes you?
- How can you make your friendship with (friend/teammate/classmate) stronger?
- What happened before (the conflict)?
- Was there something else your child could do besides (the conflict)?
- What can you do to thank (name of person)?
- How can you make (name of person) feel better?
- How can we help people less fortunate than us?
- That guy seems like he needs a helping hand. What can we do?
- What volunteer activities do you think you would enjoy?

Encourage Curiosity

DURING YOUR CHILDREN'S LIFE THERE will be moments where his current path will not lead him to the desired goal. It's precisely during these situations that curiosity will save them. Curiosity is that magical ingredient that allows your children to explore alternatives by asking "what if" questions. The answers to these questions will lead to solutions to their obstacles. They may even lead to a new and more promising path. The tools and techniques in this chapter will teach you how to develop curiosity in your kids.

Mourad is a kid who gets frustrated when things don't work out. Sure, he gets really excited when he starts a new activity but inevitably things get harder or just plain boring to him. His excitement wanes and he becomes disinterested. Shortly after, he quits.

Shawn is a boy who is interested in many things at once. He has a surface knowledge of many areas but mastery of none. He is quick to answer questions about the many areas he is dabbling with but when asked a more thoughtful question, he is often stumped. This leads to frustration and sometimes a loss of interest in the subject.

Steps you can take

- Build their sense of curiosity in commonplace situations by asking "Why do you think this happened?"

- Provide practical activities to learn by exploring in depth various topics they are interested in
- Guide them in exploring alternative opportunities to problems
- Instill a love of learning about new and unfamiliar things
- Have them try doing a routine familiar process a different way

Applications in the real world

Mourad's frustration at the moment was with writing. He would sit down to write but be overwhelmed by the blank page in front of him. He could stare at it for an hour and nothing would come. It was frustrating. His mom started by asking him questions such as "Why do you think it's so hard to start writing?" After some thought, he said "I can't think of a topic to write about!" Next, Mourad and his mom explored some alternatives such as brainstorming potential topics and entering various potential topic ideas into a search engine to see which results sparked interest. Since his habit was to write after school, they explored writing at different times of day, morning and after dinner. It turned out that Mourad's best time to write was as soon as he woke up. Brainstorming topics resulted in a short list of ideas which he readily adopted. Writing was now no longer a frustration but a pleasure.

Shawn's most recent passion was the United States political system. It was an electoral year and he was fascinated by the debates, ads, and the various talk shows surrounding the presidential candidates. Since this can be a complex and nuanced topic, Shawn's head began to swim and he started losing interest. His dad circumvented this by keeping his interest alive. He took Shawn on a trip to the Constitution Center in Philadelphia as well as a tour of Washington D.C. They discussed the steps that candidates have to take to get elected. They even explored alternative political styles (England, Italy, and Russia) on the internet. Shawn became much more knowledgeable and political science became a passion instead of a passing curiosity.

QUESTIONS TO ASK YOUR KIDS

- Why do you think (object of curiosity) works this way?
- How can (object of curiosity) work well?
- Why do you think (name of person) said this?
- How does (situation) benefit (name of person)?
- After doing an activity or a topic they were interested in: What did you like most about (activity/topic)?
- What did you like least about (activity/topic)?
- Did you discover anything new about (activity/topic)?
- Would you be interested in more information about (activity/topic)?
- You seem to have hit an obstacle. Do you have any ideas how you can overcome it?
- What would happen if we did (suggestion) to overcome your obstacle?
- If we did (possible solution), would it create a problem somewhere else?
- Wow! Can you believe we can try (new/unfamiliar activity)! Would you be interested?
- I understand that you're a little apprehensive to try something new. Would you be ok if we did it together?
- Do you think you could learn something from trying (new activity)?
- You've been doing (familiar task) for a while now. Let's play a game. How many ways can you think of to do (familiar task) better?

Figure Out Who They Really Are

TRUE PERSEVERANCE REQUIRES KIDS TO know what is important to them. They need to have core values that guide them. Just as support beams hold up a building in times of wind, these values will hold your kids steady in rough times. They will also ensure that their goals are aligned with who they truly are. The tools and steps in this chapter will assist you in guiding them.

Maria has found her passion for politics by being on the school council. She is enjoying the debates and different issues but is also unsure on which side of the fence she should be sitting on some of them. This is causing her to waver in her resolve to remain a member of the student government.

Mark's older brother sneaks cigarettes from his dad. Mark sees this happen on a regular basis and this makes him unsure of what to do. On one hand, he doesn't want to get his brother in trouble, on the other he knows stealing is wrong.

Steps you can take

- Let them figure out who they are on their own. Give them space, don't hover.
- If they ask for help, ask open ended questions about their beliefs
- Help them gain deep knowledge of topics they care about

- If they are unsure which side of a particular viewpoint they are on, ask them to read up on a variety
  of views. This will help provide answers, confirm
  their belief, and understand the other side of the
  story.
- Have conversations about morality and ethics

Applications in the real world

Maria's parents wanted to be "helicopters", hovering around
giving her advice but they held back. They allowed her to stay
in her room for an afternoon where she was able to reflect
on how she felt about the issues and her time on the school
council. As someone from a family with diabetes history, she
felt very strongly against availability of high sugar snacks
in the school vending machine. Maria then took the time to
research the topic, including many opposing viewpoints to
formulate her own unique opinion. She then argued success-
fully against these sugary snacks at the next student council
meeting. Through petitions and meetings with the principal,
the snacks were removed.

Mark's parents had no clue that their older son was pilfering
cigarettes right under their nose. What brought this to light is
their routine of weekly one to one talks with their kids. During
one of these talks, they noticed Mark was very shy and didn't
speak much. They asked him and he told them that there is
something wrong but he couldn't tell them. They spoke with
him about doing the right thing and even provided examples
from their own lives. Mark finally told them about his older brother. By doing so, he learned a valuable lesson that by
doing the right thing he can help someone else from causing
harm to himself and others.

QUESTIONS TO ASK YOUR KIDS

- What makes you excited?
- What makes you happy?
- What makes you sad?
- What do you believe?

- What do you have strong feelings about and how does it relate to your life?
- What do you think about often?
- I know you are passionate about (activity). What are the things you like most about it?
- How can I help you get to know more about (topic)?
- I found out a lot of interesting information about (topic). Would you like to read about it?
- You spent a lot of time learning about (controversial topic). What are the main points of the people supporting (controversial topic)?
- What are the main points of the people opposing (controversial topic)?
- Which position do you agree with?
- Why do you agree with this position?
- You believe that (name of person) did something wrong. Why do you believe this?
- What do you think is the right thing to do about (controversial situation)?
- Although the (controversial situation) is against your beliefs, do you think it's right to push your beliefs on (name of person)?

Make a Plan

So far, we went through many steps to develop the building blocks of your children's ability to persevere and develop a strong character, i.e. grit! Now we will concentrate on the process for having him or her achieve their actual goals. The steps in this chapter will guide you in helping your kids develop SMART goals.

Joe's passion is science. He is obsessed with practical applications such as how gravity works and astronomy. In class however, his grades need a significant boost for him to pursue a science career one day.

Martina wants the latest and coolest mobile phone. The phone costs a lot of money, of course. It's more than she has in her account and her parents are not about to buy it for her.

Sophia is an avid ballroom dancer. She practices hard but wants to make sure she moves to the next level and can effectively have a shot at winning the national competition.

Steps you can take

- Make the goal setting exercise a collaborative effort. Sit down with your children and jump in only when asked.
- Tell your children that they own this process; that they are in charge. It's very important that the goal is meaningful to them. Explain that the most

important part is that they make effort to achieve their goals, not the goal itself.

- To jump start the process, you may want to share how you planned for and achieved a goal. Also, you may want to ask your children how they already use goal-setting techniques such as saving for a toy or getting to the next level in a video game. Some of these techniques may apply to this exercise.
- Start with a benefit statement. This is what your children are striving to achieve. Ask them how it will feel to succeed and get this benefit? Then have them write it down.
- Guide them in breaking down the benefit into bite size chunks (goals). Each goal should be SMART; Specific, Measurable, Achievable, Realistic, and Time-bound
- Think small when it comes to breaking down goals. What do your children want to do tomorrow, next week, next month? These will be the tasks required to achieve the goal.
- Create a milestone in the plan. This is a task where your children will measure progress against the plan.
- Post the resulting plan in a visible place such as a refrigerator or their room door. The idea here is that your children should pass these goals several times a day.

Applications in the real world

Joe's mom, a medical doctor, shared how she achieved her childhood passion for learning anatomy. She briefly discussed some steps she took. Then she sat down with Joe and guided him in creating the plan below.

BENEFIT	Feel great about getting excellent grades in science so that I can get into advanced classes and have a chance at a science career
GOAL	Raise grades to A by the end of the spring semester

Task	Planned end date or timeframe
List subjects where grades should be higher	This Saturday
Spend an extra 30 minutes each day to read textbooks for troubled subjects	For two months every day
Speak with science teacher to get opinion on how to raise grades	Next Monday
Milestone – check grades	End of the month

Martina's mom reminded her of the time she was younger and wanted a new bike. Martina was able to do chores,
babysitting, and selling her unwanted items to raise money
for the bike. With her mom's help, she was able to use some
of these steps in creating the plan below.

BENEFIT	Feel like I have the latest and greatest phone which lets me surf the internet fast-er and download the latest apps
GOAL	Earn enough money to buy the new phone in three months

Task	Planned end date or timeframe
Brainstorm ways to make mon-ey other than the ones below	Sunday afternoon
Act on the best ideas that come out of brainstorming	Monday afternoon
Gather used clothes and take them to local reseller	Next Friday
Do some babysitting	For a period of three months
Milestone – check funds	End of each week

Sophia's parents recognized that their daughter would need their help in creating a plan. This also required consulting her dancing coach. What resulted is the plan below.

BENEFIT   Feel like a champion!

GOAL   Place in the top 3 of the national ballroom dance competition for the next year

Task	Planned end date or timeframe
Arrange private lessons 3 times a week	Next Week
Practice after school for 45 minutes	Every other day
Attend 3 regional competitions	3 times in the next 6 months
Review taped performance with coach after every competition	3 times in the next 6 months
Adjust dance routine per feedback from coach after every lesson	Every week
Milestone – place in the top 10 of the qualifying competition leading up to nationals	In 4 months

QUESTIONS TO ASK YOUR KIDS

- What do you want to achieve (goal)?
- When do you want to achieve (goal) by?
- Can you write it down?
- What do you think it will take to achieve (goal)?
- How will your current day be impacted by trying to achieve (goal)?
- What will it mean for you to achieve (goal)?
- How would it make you feel if you didn't achieve (goal) because you didn't persevere?
- Would you like to see how I planned for (your goal)?
- Can I help you plan?
- How did you plan for (goal your child already achieved)?
- How can you break (goal) into small tasks?
- What dependencies do you have for each task?
- Does (goal) meet the SMART criteria?
- How can you get started?
- What task can you do this week?
- What are some milestones that mean you're on your way to achieving (goal)?
- Where can you write down the plan to achieve (goal)?
- Where can we put the plan so that it's visible to you every day?

Follow the Process

HAVING A PLAN IS EXTREMELY important to your children. It allows them to have a roadmap to how their dreams will be achieved. The important thing at this point is that the plan be followed or the motivation of your kids will wane. This doesn't mean that everything will go according to plan. All plans need adjusting and sometimes significantly so. The important thing for your kids to understand is that success doesn't happen by accident. It happens by constant and sustained effort and by following the process set out in the plan. This chapter provides you with the tools and techniques to do just that.

Joe started his plan with gusto by listing all of the subjects he was a little weak in (biology, chemistry). He then spent 30 minutes per day for one week studying these subjects as planned. He then started to skip a day, then two. He was supposed to speak with his science teacher on Monday but postponed it for a week.

Martina brainstormed ways to make money and came up with some useful ideas such as getting an after school job and holding a car wash. She didn't follow up on any of these ideas, however. She went back to her tried and true ways of getting cash by selling her gently used clothing and babysitting.

Sophia had no problems going to private lessons or competing regionally but she stumbled when it came time to practice after school and applying feedback from her coach to her dance routines.

Steps you can take

- Sit down with them for a regular plan review. This could be weekly or monthly depending on the children and the timeline of the plan.
- During the review, discuss with them what went right, what went wrong, and areas for improvement
- Compliment them for effort, not just success. It's the effort and following the plan that you're trying to develop. Achievement is a byproduct of that effort.
- Conversely, don't scold them for missing a target. Instead, gently coax them into thinking how they can get back on track.
- Do not offer bribes for achievement of goals.

Applications in the real world

Joe's mom scheduled a weekly progress meeting to discuss how he's doing with the plan. At the second week's meeting, it became apparent that Joe was floundering. His mom complimented him on the effort of practicing every day during the first week of the plan but didn't come down on him for where he was deficient. She asked him what he could do to resume every day practice. He replied that after school he was too tired but could try after dinner. She also encouraged him to email his teacher for an appointment thereby setting the date.

Martina's mom also had weekly reviews with her daughter. She gave her a high five for applying the money raising skills she already had and congratulated her on a fun and productive brainstorming session. She then asked why Martina never followed through on what they came up with. It turns out Martina was a little scared and overwhelmed of applying for jobs and doing a car wash. Together, Martina and her mom researched car washing fundraising on the internet and added the steps of getting it done to the plan. They also placed a task on the plan to speak to her friends about the details of applying for jobs at the local mall.

During Sophia's monthly progress review, it became apparent that her busy schedule of school, field hockey, and music was overwhelming her ability to practice every day.

After complimenting her on never missing her private dance lessons, her parents and Sophia brainstormed ways for her to practice. They came up with three days a week practice sessions. They also asked why she never applied the coach's feedback. It turned out that the coach never had time to fully explain what was wrong with Sophia's routine, making it difficult to apply. Sophia added a task to the plan to ask the coach the best way of communicating with her. The coach suggested making recorded voice overs during her taped routines. This eliminated the need for feedback sessions and provided real time commentary that Sophia could use immediately.

QUESTIONS TO ASK YOUR KIDS

- When should we sit down for our plan review?
- What's the best time to talk about the plan?
- Which tasks are you satisfied with so far?
- Which tasks do you think need more work?
- What is working so well that you can continue to do for the next tasks?
- What can you do differently to catch up on tasks?
- Do you think you're putting in enough effort to achieve (goal)?
- What is preventing you from completing the planned tasks?
- Do you think the next tasks are achievable in the timeframe you planned?

Celebrate Little Wins

DEVELOPING GRIT IS NOT EASY and even the most alluring benefits and the best laid plans can seem like a long hard slog for kids. The steps in this chapter show you how to celebrate the small steps on the ladder to their success. Remember, it's the little things that count.

Laura's goal was to run a marathon as a benefit for a cancer charity. She had trouble finishing 5k (3.1 mile) runs, however. She struggled twice before but was unable to cross the finish line.

Aaron's plan was to someday run for elected office. One of his first tasks was to become popular by meeting three new people every day. This was an ambitious plan for a shy child.

Steps you can take

- Guide your children into achieving an easy goal within a short time
- Lavish praise on your children when they leave their comfort zone. Small age appropriate risks build self-confidence and teach the important lesson that even with the possibility of failure, a risk is sometimes worth taking.
- Celebrate little victories and small steps. Make sure to point out that although small, they all lead up to their bigger goal.

Applications in the real world

During the most recent 5k run, Laura was struggling in the last mile. She was winded and tired. Her legs felt like rubber. Nonetheless, remembering her goal she was able to find a burst of energy and sprint to cross the finish line for the first time. Afterward, her parents took her out to dinner and complimented her on making the effort for the final push. Notice that it was the effort that was complimented, not the actual achievement. This provided confidence to Laura for attempting the loftier goal of running in a marathon.

Aaron was very excited about going for his goal of meeting three new people every day. That morning in school he was about to approach his first new acquaintance when he felt the butterflies in his stomach. After a few moments of hemming and hawing, he approached the student and introduced himself. He was rewarded with a smile and a new friend. That was all he could do that day. His dad praised Aaron for approaching one new person. That night they went out for ice cream. Aaron was motivated to try again and met two new people the following day. He learned that by taking a risk, he can make his goal reality.

QUESTIONS TO ASK YOUR KIDS

- Wow, you've achieved (little win)! Are you excited to move on to bigger things?
- You are doing really well at this! See what you can accomplish when you put some effort into it?
- You were uncomfortable when you tried (activity) but you see how your effort paid off. Do you feel more comfortable trying new things?
- How did it feel to succeed at something new?
- Do you see how this (little win) helps you in achieving (long term goal)?

Teach To Expect Setbacks

KIDS FREQUENTLY UNDERESTIMATE HOW DIFFICULT it can be to achieve a goal, and then they get frustrated and discouraged when they don't. If your children decide that they want to play a musical instrument, for example, encourage them but be realistic. Point out the challenges and the dedication it will require. The idea isn't to make the goal seem too out of reach, but rather to explain the seriousness of the undertaking.

Jackson was taking karate for several years now, in pursuit of his goal of getting a black belt. He was very good at it but his resolve was starting to wane as the years went on and he was repeating similar moves over and over.

Melanie wants to learn how to swim competitively. This is a struggle as she has to drag herself out early morning to practice. She spends endless hours in the cold pool and as she gets more advanced, the competition is getting tougher. Over the past few months, she has placed at the bottom of several competitions.

Steps you can take

- Tell them where you succeeded and where you failed to reach your goals. Make sure to explain the effort and grit that success required. Convey how long it took to achieve the goal or how long it took to realize the goal is unachievable.

- Allow your children to overcome challenges independently. Be a coach, not the problem solver.
- Be upfront about what you are teaching your children. Explain to them that they are working on developing perseverance skills and that struggle is likely and failure is possible.
- Convey to your children that they own the success as well as the failure of going for a particular goal. It's not always in their power to succeed but it is always within his control to apply effort.
- Make your children understand that setbacks are expected. It's the ability to rebound from them that is the difference between success and failure.
- Be there for you kids when they struggle or fail. Provide support, assist them in evaluating why things went wrong, and guide them in re-planning.
- Help them overcome procrastination. It's easy for your children to escape into video games, shopping, over-eating to avoid taking on the difficult tasks needed to achieve their goals.

Applications in the real world

Jackson's dad used to take martial arts when he was a child. He related to Jackson how it was easy at first and then got progressively harder. His instructor was getting more demanding with the little things and Jackson's dad was tempted to give up. He confided in Jackson that he didn't give up because of his goal of reaching black belt and being able to stand up to school bullies. This made him persevere for several years until the coveted black belt was his. He told his son that although they share the same goal, it was Jackson's decision on how to proceed but that he would be there for him as a coach and to lend him all the support he needed. The thing that mattered most of all is that Jackson apply all the effort that he can muster.

Melanie's mom was not athletic at all but realized that Melanie would be very upset in the long term if she didn't pursue competitive swimming. On the way to school, she asked her "What else could you try that may get better results?" or

"I think you can definitely be a strong competitor. How else can you solve the problem of getting up in the morning for practice? What can you change or do differently that would make you a better competitor?" Melanie came up with several options including cutting down her time hanging out with friends which was distracting her. Melanie also started sleeping earlier so she could be alert for practice. The results became apparent. In a period of several months, she won two competitions. It was an important lesson in rebounding from failure.

QUESTIONS TO ASK YOUR KIDS

- Did I ever tell you how I achieved (a goal you achieved)?
- Did I ever tell you why I tried but failed (goal you failed)?
- That (task) didn't go so well. What do you think you can do to overcome the obstacle(s) in your way?
- What advice would you like from me to overcome (obstacle)?
- Your goal will require a lot of effort. How can I help you overcome (obstacle)?
- Would you like to share with me your strategy for overcoming obstacles?
- What can you do today to move your goal along?
- You seem to be struggling with (task). Would you like to talk about it?
- Sometimes things don't go as planned. Can we sit down today and see how we can make it right?
- Putting (task) off until tomorrow is the same as delaying your goal for one more day. What time today can you start (task)?

Get Them to Apply Lessons Learned

ONE OF THE KEY TAKEAWAYS from a setback is to review what went wrong and determine what could have been done differently in that situation. Better still, these lessons can be applied to other similar situations. Even the review process itself is useful as it teaches your kids critical thinking skills that they can use in school, home, and eventually work. Finding and applying lessons learned will increase their grit as they gain confidence in their ability to overcome obstacles in a systematic way. The steps in this chapter will help you teach them how to analyze and apply these lessons.

John competes in spelling bees. He's passionate about words and memorizes new words every night. His goal is to be national champion. Lately, he was stumped at a regional contest and came in second. He is determined to learn from his mistake.

Sheena trusted her friends that she had a crush on a boy at school. She shared how much they had in common and his favorite things to do. This backfired as one of them used the information to ask the boy out herself. Sheena was understandably hurt and never wanted this to happen again.

Steps you can take

- Help them recognize that something went wrong. Human beings are very good at self-delusion. This leads to denial that something has gone amiss. Your children needs to know that a mistake happened and he needs to think about it.

- Guide them in analyzing what went wrong. Write down what led up to the setback and what actually happened. Due to the emotional charge of admitting to a mistake, it may be helpful to get additional viewpoints on the issue.
- Discuss with them what lessons they can draw from the setback. Ask lots of questions to make sure they understand the lesson.

Applications in the real world

John acknowledged his mistake right away. He sat down with his dad and they penned down possible causes for the misspelling. Once they had written down everything they could think of, they rated each one from 1 to 10 with 10 being most likely and 1 being least likely. The reason that came up on top is that the word's origin is French, a language that John was unfamiliar with. After applying some brainstorming techniques, John realized that he should study rules of several languages in order to understand likely pronunciations of unfamiliar words.

Sheena did not want to admit that she did anything wrong. She blamed the other girl for stealing her would-be boyfriend. It took her mom several talks and questions to make her acknowledge her role in what happened. To get additional insight, Sheena spoke with another friend who knew the story. Once her head was clear, she knew the lesson here is to not reveal too much and place too much trust in people. Unfortunately, sometimes friends turn out to be false. She has also figured out that this lesson applies to other relationships in her life. She has applied it ever since.

QUESTIONS TO ASK YOUR KIDS

- Do you think things are going as planned?
- Are you getting closer to (goal)?
- Would you like to talk about how things are going with (goal)?

- What have you learned from (mistake)?
- When can we sit down and write down what went wrong?
- Sometimes it takes someone with a different viewpoint to look at what happened. Who else can you speak with to get a different perspective on what went wrong?
- What can you do differently next time?
- Can anything be done now to accomplish (task)?
- Is there any other area to which the lesson can be applied?
- Where can we place the lesson learned so it's easily available for you to read?

Guide in Decision Making

MAKING DECISIONS WILL BE A large part of your kids' lives, like it or not. A key component to them being able to develop grit and persevere in their goals is to be able to evaluate and make smart, rational decisions. This chapter provides you with the steps to guide them in the decision making process.

Mercedes had a big decision to make. She had to decide whether to attend her local school in an underserved area or get up early morning to attend a magnet school two hours away.

Colleen's decision was not as drastic but was important to her. She had been playing tennis for many years and has put in a lot of blood, sweat, and tears to have a shot of being a star on her high school squad. Lately however, she has been ambivalent about tennis. She recently got hooked on acting and wanted to devote more time to it but couldn't because of her tennis commitments. Which path should she choose?

Steps you can take

- Encourage decision-making by letting your kids make choices on their own. Provide them with several options and ask which ones they would like to take?
- Teach them to carefully weigh the options in order to choose the best way forward. It's important to emphasize that taking shortcuts will not get them to their goal faster but are likely to set them back.

- Use stories from actual people or fictional characters to illustrate how they solved a similar problem.
- Help them find people who have solved this problem before. Discuss how the problem was solved with them and if the solution applies to the situation. Carefully evaluate every piece of advice however, to make sure it's not biased in any way.

Applications in the real world

Mercedes' mom wanted to guide her daughter but also to make sure that her daughter was making her own choice. She assisted her in making a spreadsheet on the computer where they carefully wrote down all the pros and cons for staying in her current school versus attending the charter school. She then left Mercedes alone to mull over the decision. Her mom told her daughter not to rush as this was a potentially life changing decision. After two weeks of deliberations, Mercedes was still not ready. She consulted with a friend who made a choice to stay and an acquaintance who is going to the charter school. Only after this did Mercedes make her choice; the charter school.

Colleen sought her inspiration from famous athletes that have quit sports to pursue other interests. Being a tennis fan, she read the story of Elena Dementieva, a 29 year old star who retired being ranked #9 in the world in order to start a family. She was equally inspired by Bjorn Borg, a tennis player in the 70s and 80s who won 11 grand slam titles. He retired at age 26 because he lost his competitive drive, his passion for the sport. She also spoke with a former high school star that quit in her sophomore year to pursue another sport. After much deliberation and with a final consultation with her parents, she did quit tennis and is happily pursuing her acting talents.

QUESTIONS TO ASK YOUR KIDS

- What do you think your choices are in this situation?
- Which of these choices look the most promising?
- Which of these choices do you feel most confident about?

- Here are some options that might work. Which of these would you like to explore?
- You've narrowed down your options, great! Have you compared them against each other?
- What are the benefits of (option)?
- What are the drawbacks of (option)?
- Are there any dependencies for (option) that may slow you down?
- Will (option) truly bring you closer to your goal?
- There is (actual person/fictional character) that went through a similar situation. Would you like to learn how they did it?
- You've spoken with (person who solved the problem). What do you think applies to you?
- You've spoken with (person who solved the problem). Do you think (person) told you the whole story?

Stick to what's Really Important

IT WILL BE DIFFICULT FOR your kids to be resilient and reach for their goals. There may even be ethical dilemmas that confuse them. Many distractions and competing priorities will be present, opening them up to aimlessly flop from one activity to another. A strong commitment to their true self and their real goals can help. In a previous chapter, you helped them figure out who they really are. This chapter allows you to help them keep their eye straight on the prize ahead while being true to themselves.

Mark is an avid sport player who is involved in soccer, football, and baseball. His goal is to get on the school team for all three. As he got older, he witnessed a number of teammates experimenting with performance enhancement drugs. He has stayed away so far, but as more teammates become better athletes while on drugs, he is tempted.

Emily is passionate about acting and is in the school play. The play is funny but some of her fellow actors want to make it raunchier with skin tight and see through outfits. This does not sit well with Emily's conservative religious beliefs.

Steps you can take

- Teach them to listen to their conscience. It will guide them in the ethical dilemmas that will come up.

- Show them meditation techniques if you know how. Meditation clears up the mind and allows them to focus.
- Talk to them about ethics and morality. If you or your children are religious, you may want to discuss a story from your religion. If not, find and relate a story from history.
- Help them start a journal to write down their thoughts and feelings

Applications in the real world

Mark wrote regularly in a journal for two years. He described on paper how his teammates started and continued to take performance enhancing drugs. He wrote how conflicted he felt. On one hand, it was wrong. On the other, these boys won games! His mom, a yoga instructor, taught him meditation techniques which he applied to clear his mind of clutter and to openly consider his options. He realized that he would be very disappointed with himself if he took drugs even if he got better at sports. The next time he was offered some, he decidedly said no.

Emily mentioned to her mom her reluctance to bare skin. She related to her parents how it was tough to reconcile modern norms and her cultural upbringing. Emily understood what her fellow actors wanted but her conscience was against it. Together, Emily and her parents read and discussed several stories from their religious teachings. They also talked about conscientious objectors during wars that abstain from fighting based on their beliefs. Emily decided to participate in the play after all, but not as an actress. She helped with set design and script editing instead.

QUESTIONS TO ASK YOUR KIDS

- What do you think is the right thing to do?
- Do you feel comfortable doing (controversial situation)?
- What makes you uneasy in doing (controversial situation)?

- What do you think your next move should be in (controversial situation)?
- Would you like to learn to think deeply about (controversial situation)?
- You've meditated or thought deeply about (controversial situation). What do you think your actions should be?
- What would (religious figure/historical figure) do in a similar situation?
- What makes (controversial situation) different from what the (religious figure/historical figure) has faced?
- What makes (controversial situation) similar to what the (religious figure/historical figure) has faced?
- This true story I read is remarkably similar to what you're facing. Are there any lessons you can use for your situation?
- Would you like to write down your thoughts or feelings so you can reflect on them later?
- Have you reviewed your journal for any insights into what you're facing now?

Show Them How You Do It

As the mom or dad for your children, you are the well from which they get inspiration. No matter how rocky your relationship with your kids may be at any given time, they will look to you for support and guidance. Showing your children how you have persevered, are persevering, and will persevere is a powerful tool for them to model resilience and grit. This chapter provides the steps to achieve this goal.

Daniel's dad is a project manager whose goal it is to make sure his family is taken care of financially. To do this, he has committed himself to a lifetime of learning and self-improvement. His goal is to inspire the same in his son.

Brock's mom and dad own a martial arts school and teaches the same in the local YMCA. His dad also has a full time construction business to run. They went through some ups and downs in their business and school but have shown grit in persevering through the different issues. This can be a model for their son.

Steps you can take

- Tell them about goals you have achieved or those you failed to achieve. Answer any questions, even the tough ones. The tough questions are what makes them understand the struggle.

- Tell them about what you're trying to do now. Explain the issues and decisions to be made. Clearly show how you're going about making them.
- Tell them about the challenges of tomorrow. Describe how you're planning to tackle them.

Applications in the real world

Daniel's parents have a family tradition of a weekly meeting where everyone gets to discuss the important things in their lives. Daniel's dad discussed how he tackled public speaking. This was a challenge that took three years of consistent Toastmasters meetings and ten completed speeches to earn a competent communicator certificate. He described how he solved a particular challenge of picking the topic of a speech. He told Daniel that it was tough going at first until he was inspired to pick topics he was passionate about. That provided a pool of speeches that practically wrote themselves. Speaking about things that mattered to him, provided Daniel's dad with the motivation to persevere through the years to complete his goal. His new challenge is mastering internet marketing, a daunting task, the plan for which he shared with his son.

Brock's parents described their struggles in the financial crisis which hit them in their martial arts and construction businesses. This double whammy almost bankrupted them. They sought guidance from their religion and decided to hold on to what they had. They started with a plan to build the martial arts school into several locations with heavy word of mouth advertising. They adjusted class times and sizes so that students got their money's worth and referred more students. The plan for the construction business was to go after the high end market. This worked slowly but favorably over the past few years. The challenge in the months and years ahead is for Brock's parents to grow their school at several locations by hiring teachers and grow the construction business by showcasing their work to high end home owners.

QUESTIONS TO ASK YOUR KIDS

- I've told you about how I achieved (your goal). Are there any questions you would like to ask?
- I've failed at achieving (your goal). I think my failure is due to (reason). Are there any similarities to your situation?
- Right now, I'm making an effort to achieve (your goal). I'm doing (tasks) to make it happen. I'm having a hard time with (obstacles) but here is what I'm doing about it. Would you like to learn more?
- Next, I'm planning on achieving (goal). Here is my plan of action. I think some tasks will be easy while others will be hard because of (obstacles). Can you sit with me and help figure out a way to overcome them?

Take Care of Their Health

KEEPING YOUR KIDS HEALTHY IS not only an important part of being a parent, it plays a crucial part in her ability to get through challenging times and tough it out to achieve her goals. Anyone who showed up sick with the flu to take a year end school exam can attest to that. The steps in this chapter will help you guide your child to a strong body and mind that will serve as the shield for rocky moments.

David likes his sugar. He grazes nutritious foods but loves to munch on candies, pretzels, and cookies. This keeps him alert for hours and prevents him from getting a good night sleep. This in turn, makes him forgetful about school and home responsibilities.

Olivia can be glued to the computer for hours at a time. She will move only to go to the bathroom or to get something to eat. She is at risk of becoming obese and it's getting hard for her to keep up with her friends at school or gym class. She is also starting to develop a negative body image which makes her mom very concerned.

Steps you can take

- Tell them the importance of getting a good night's sleep. Most kids need at least seven hours and teenagers need close to nine. Make sure they hear your message and do your best to enforce it.

- Show them how to eat a nutritious diet. Avoid processed foods (bologna, hot dogs, and chips) by substituting un-processed options (grilled pork, steak, baked potatoes). Fill them up on fruits and vegetables; fresh is best but frozen or canned will do fine in most cases.
- Encourage them to exercise. This doesn't mean that they need to join a gym or start running marathons. Any movement such as biking, backyard baseball games, or doing house hold chores will keep them moving.
- Teach them relaxation techniques. Meditation and/ or yoga are wonderful ways in which they can focus on their goals and calm themselves down after a setback.

Applications in the real world

David's parents set a bed time guide line for him. They wanted him to be in bed by 9:30. They related several scenarios where lack of sleep causes him to be absent minded in school and have a lack of energy in sports. To combat the sugar problem, they placed a small snack bag where he could place about 3-4 snack size candy bars. David could pick from this bag the entire day until 2 hours before bed time. Once the candies ran out, no more sugar was given. Once 7pm rolled around, the bag was put away. After one week, David's parents noticed a difference. After one month, his test scores improved and he became a more responsible child which in turn helped him focus on his goals.

Olivia and her mom got into the habit of walking after school. They took 30 minutes to walk around their neighborhood. When the winter months arrived, they started walking at the local mall. Her mom also guided Olivia in reading a quick book on meditation and kept her motivated by trying it out with her. They did a quick 5 minute relaxation technique every day before school and on the weekends. She also instituted a no PC hour one hour before bed. Instead, they discussed current events. All of these changes inspired Olivia to get perspective and become interested in the outside world again. She became more active and started hanging out with her friends more.

QUESTIONS TO ASK YOUR KIDS

- You look tired this morning. Did you get enough sleep?
- You are having difficulty in finishing your homework. Why don't you go to sleep 30 minutes earlier today?
- Do you think you would feel less sleepy if you went to bed an hour earlier than yesterday?
- You feel groggy this afternoon. Do you think the bag of chips you had for lunch had something to do with it?
- Why don't you try apple chips instead of potato chips for snack today?
- Let's try these carrots instead of pretzels. How were they? Did you miss the pretzels? (ask after your children come home)
- Why don't you help me with (household chore) this afternoon? We can make a game of who can do it faster.
- What sport would you like to play during the year or summer?
- Would you like to play (outdoor game) with me after school?
- I'm going running before dinner. Would you like to join me?
- I'm going to be doing yoga after lunch and I could use a workout partner. Can you practice with me?
- Yoga can help you focus and relax. Would you like to learn how?
- You had a rough day. Why don't you go to your room to relax and take some deep breaths?

Conclusion

THANK YOU AGAIN FOR READING this book!

"I can do it!", "I will do it!",
"Thanks for your help, mom and dad!"

These are the words I sincerely believe your kids will say after you have started applying the concepts in this book.

I am confident that the ideas in this book have provided you with the tools you need to guide you kids to develop grit through passion, personal improvement, planning, and learning from mistakes.

Throughout their lives, your daughter or son will encounter many different opportunities and challenges. Please refer back to this book to get new insights to apply to each individual situation. One day, they will grow up and become a parent. They will look back at you for inspiration and hopefully apply these steps to their children too.

My wife and I are also excited as we watch our sons grow up with grit so that they can fulfill their dreams!

For much more information about the topics of grit and parenting, inside information on upcoming books, as well as many free giveaways please SIGN UP at www.LeeDavidDaniels.com. It doesn't cost a thing!

Finally, if you enjoyed this book, then I'd like to ask you for a favor, would you be kind enough to leave a review for this book on Amazon? It is really helpful for me to make sure this book is the best it can be. It will be greatly appreciated!

Good luck!   *Lee David Daniels*

www.LeeDavidDaniels.com

Learning More – Additional Resources

WHILE THE CONTENTS OF THIS book provide you with a rich and robust toolkit to encourage success in your kids, there is much more to learn. The resources below are those that I personally use regularly to raise my boys. Please dive in and explore!

Books

- Grit: The Power of Passion and Perseverance – Angela Duckworth
- Mindset: The New Psychology of Success – Carol S. Dweck
- How to Talk So Kids Will Listen & Listen So Kids Will Talk – Adele Faber and Elaine Mazlish
- The Whole-Brain Child: 12 Revolutionary Strategies to Nurture Your Child's Developing Mind – Daniel J. Siegel and Tina Payne Bryson
- Peaceful Parent, Happy Kids: How to Stop Yelling and Start Connecting – Laura Markham
- Free Yourself from Anger: A Do-it-Yourself Manual for Anger Junkies – Terry Erle Clayton
- Smart Parenting for Smart Kids: Nurturing Your Child's True Potential – Eileen Kennedy-Moore and Mark S. Lowenthal

Blogs

- *https://getconnectdad.com/* – parents writing for other parents on various topics but centered around 52 traits to develop in kids
- *http://greatergood.berkeley.edu/raising_happiness/* – great insights into various parenting topics
- *http://parentingchaos.com/* – a very popular blog with stories of struggle, challenges we strive to overcome, and moments of embracing our children through play
- *www.kidsinthehouse.com/* – thousands of videos on parenting topics
- *https://www.fatherville.com/* – great tips for dads

About the Author

LEE DAVID DANIELS IS A #1 bestselling author who helps with topics that focus on parenting, relationships, and career improvement. He believes that success in these areas is achievable by anyone as long as consistent action is taken with the goal of persevering despite all obstacles.

Lee resides in Bucks County PA, USA where he spends most of his time writing, being happily married for over 20 years, and raising two boys. In his spare time, he enjoys skiing, martial arts, and cooking. With a deep passion for helping others, building life skills, and inspiring others to take charge of their lives, he is committed to a path of consistent and life-long self-improvement.

But that's not all! The blog at www.LeeDavidDaniels.com contains tons of valuable and practical tips and techniques that you can put to use immediately. Sign up today and get bonus materials such as real life grit examples, downloaded blog posts, additional resources, and much, much more!

He can be found on:

Facebook – https://www.facebook.com/leedaviddanielsauthor/
Twitter – https://twitter.com/leeddaniels
Website – www.leedaviddaniels.com
Email – lee@leedaviddaniels.com

www.LeeDavidDaniels.com

Made in United States
Orlando, FL
03 December 2021

11077632R10061